JEFFREY PATNAUDE

The Kingdom of FROG

Illustrated by
BONNIE ZACHERLE

LifeRich Publishing is a registered trademark of The Reader's Digest Association, Inc.

LifeRich Publishing books may be ordered through booksellers or by contacting:

LifeRich Publishing
1663 Liberty Drive
Bloomington, IN 47403
www.liferichpublishing.com
1 (888) 238-8637

ISBN: 978-1-4897-2897-5 (hc)
ISBN: 978-1-4897-2839-5 (sc)
ISBN: 978-1-4897-2840-1 (e)

Print information available on the last page.

LifeRich Publishing rev. date: 05/27/2020

DEDICATION

To the two little Frogs of my Kingdom:

Scooper and Skunk

"The most sacred of sanctuaries is within the cathedrals of a child's mind."

Jeffrey Patnaude © 2016

INTRODUCTION

The child's mind is the source of great creativity and endless ideas. And when listening to their interpretation of what they think adults have said, it often becomes the source of great entertainment.

Our Father, who art in Heaven, **Howard** *be thy Name.* That is how the God Frog was named Howard. It sounded exactly correct to a child's mind - and so it was - and it was good.

"And He walks with me, and he talks with me"... this is a line from the classic Hymn, ***In the Garden.*** That was how **Andy,** the Jesus character arrived: "Andy walks with me, Andy talks with me"...

Sophie, from the name Sophia, is a character throughout history who represents Wisdom - and here she remains constant to her name. Able to hear the true message in the teachings of Andy, she becomes the first follower and represents a disciple of Jesus, Mary Magdalene.

Long ago, before there was any sound in the forest or movement in any of the ponds, there was one old frog who sat on a high ledge far above all that was below. Howard was a magnificent frog. Though old, he was strong and very wise from his many years of age.

Each day and each night, he sat and watched the sway of the trees and the light that shone on the ponds. He was pleased with the beauty that lay below him. But something was missing. The sound of living things was not there! He wanted to hear the croaking that a frog makes when singing or the "Ribbet, Ribbet" when frogs talk, the "Crock, Crock" that frogs make when they play or the "Croak, Croak" when they want attention.

So Howard decided to call out in his loudest Croak to see if there would be an answer. Moving to the highest point on the ledge, he took the deepest breath, expanded his large lungs and called out: "CROAK, CROAK, CROAK." He listened for a response, but there was none. He tried again, in an even bigger voice. This time he heard a reply.

"Ribbet, Ribbet" said the voice. Howard was so excited that he called out again: "CROAK, CROAK, CROAK." And he heard again; "Ribbet, Ribbet." Then, more voices: "Crock, Crock", "Revvit, Revvit." And "Croac, Croac" was another. Soon many, many frogs came to the ponds, life was full of songs and play - and it was good.

Howard was very happy now to sit upon his high perch and watch the excitement in the ponds below. The frogs would jump from lily pads to floating logs as they played tag and croaked with happy voices. Some just sat in the sun and warmed themselves while others searched for food to fill their already big tummies. They were so happy that they had answered the Croak that called them to these beautiful ponds, just like a kingdom – a Kingdom of Frog.

Life in The Kingdom of Frog was so beautiful that every frog felt like they had never felt before. They played with each other and felt joyful. They jumped higher than ever before, ate more than they had in their lifetime and slept all through the night until the light of the morning sun would tickle their eyes to wake them up to enjoy another day in The Kingdom of Frog.

But something started to happen that would upset the life in the Kingdom. The frogs began to multiply so quickly that they had to spread out to other ponds for more room, far from the first pond from where they began.

When they got too far away from Howard and his voice that called them from the beginning, they started to forget about the ways of the Kingdom. They began to argue about who was the greenest, which ones could sing out the loudest or jump the furthest. So they divided into many groups to protect themselves from the frogs who were different and no longer like them.

Howard felt sad watching the frogs divide among themselves because they feared each other. He had called them to be kind to all others, to respect those who were not like them and to love one another as one family. But that was not happening now. Instead, they built walls of mud around their groups for protection and stood guard because they were afraid.

Howard knew what he must do. He would choose one Frog as a teacher to go to all of the groups of frogs and try to reunite them into the one Kingdom again. And Andy was just that Frog.

Andy had walked with him and talked with him after the calling to all frogs and that is how Howard had gotten to know and love Andy. He was a frog unlike all the others as he had a special nature that Howard knew would be the example of a quality he had imagined for all frogs.

Howard talked to Andy about his concern of the frogs dividing into groups that were at unrest with one another. He told him that they needed someone to teach them not to be afraid, to come out from behind their mud walls and learn to live together again. Howard put his big webbed foot on Andy's young forehead and told him to go out and teach all that he had learned in The Kingdom of Frog.

Andy had a hard time at first as he had not done this before. He went to the first pond where the Kingdom began and he called for all the frogs to come to him to hear a story.

The frogs all leapt from their pads and logs and came and sat in front of Andy wondering what he was about to say. He began with a story:

"Once there was a young frog who asked his Master: "Why am I here?" The Master replied: "You are here to answer just one question and with that answer, you will understand everything else you will need to know."

"What is the question?" asked the young frog.

The Master replied: "Why are you here?"

The young frog went away confused. The answer he received was a question. Was the answer to his question to be found in the same question?

All of the frogs who listened to the story were also confused. Some laughed nervously as they did not understand. Others shrieked at Andy and told him to go away. Some threw stones at him because they didn't like him.

But there was one frog who was not confused. Her name was Sophie. She liked his story and knew that she would follow Andy wherever he would go. When he spoke, she felt a feeling deep inside her frog belly that was like a fire. She knew that one day she would teach, just like Andy did.

Andy continued to speak to the crowds as Howard had requested:

To the frogs who had moved far away from the pond and lived behind mud walls Andy said:

"The pathway back to the Kingdom is by the path of love, not fear. And once the light of this truth is lit within you, nothing can blow it out."

To the frogs who were so lazy and never played or jumped but instead just sat on a log he said:

"Do not be satisfied with only what you are now or let others define you. Instead celebrate who you are becoming. The Kingdom of Frog is within you. It burns like a bright light waiting for the curtain to be pulled back so that all others can be enlightened by the light within."

The frogs understood nothing Andy said so they just closed their eyes and went back to sleep. A few chirped and snorted but it sounded like they had just returned to their slumber.

Some of the older frogs got together in a group to challenge Andy. They did not like a younger frog acting like he had answers to what, for them, had become hard questions. They gathered around him as he came to a part of the pond where the Temple Trees grew. These trees were tall and beautiful and provided shade for the frogs on hot days. That is why the elder frogs claimed this area as they felt superior to all of the other frogs.

"Who are you to try and tell us what we are to do with our frog lives?" they asked Andy. Are you some warrior who thinks he can wield a sword and cut away the comfort of the shadow of the trees and the luxury of how we live?

"The sword I carry only cuts away the old beliefs that you must release," he replied. *"What is true will overcome even those who live in darkness."*

The elder frogs did not like what he was saying. They felt that he was suggesting that they were the ones "living in darkness" when instead, they only enjoyed the shade of the big Temple Trees.

"Go away," they started to shout at him. "You are not wanted here and we do not want your message."

Andy responded one more time before leaving: *"Wherever you find truth, embrace it with all your hearts and it will give you strength."*

"What is truth?" cried out the eldest frog of all. The rest of the crowd just laughed but Andy didn't need to respond as he already knew that all that he was teaching was true.

Andy was not surprised at this reaction. It had been the same in most parts of the Kingdom. But he did remember those frog faces that smiled at his message or the frog legs that reached out to touch him from the crowd. There were many, he guessed who had heard the message and there was that one frog Sophie who he knew believed.

Sophie stayed in the back of the crowd so that she could watch the reaction of the other frogs who listened to Andy. She believed in her little frog heart that everything that he was saying was true and that the Kingdom would be such a happier place if only others believed too.

"The Kingdom of Frog is open to everyone who follows the pathway home" was something Andy had said that she repeated in her frog brain. *"What you are seeking is that by which you will be known"* was another comment Andy made which she could not get out of her mind. These were messages that all frogs had to understand. And she now knew *what* she was seeking and *how* she would become known. She was ready to begin.

When Sophie returned to the pond where Howard lived high above on his perch she became disturbed by what she saw. A crowd of frogs had circled around Andy and were spitting on him and throwing stones at him. Frightened for Andy, Sophie ran toward the crowd to try to stop them but she could not get through because so many frogs were now turning against Andy and his message. They pushed him toward the edge of a high cliff and told him to leave The Kingdom of Frog forever.

Andy did not show any fear like those in the crowd. Instead he just smiled and began to speak one last time.

"You have listened but not heard the message that I was sent to bring to you. It is a message about love, not fear – about caring for each other, not competing. You do not need to build walls to keep others out – instead you are to build bridges to welcome the stranger in. Do not look for the answers to your lives outside but instead, all answers lie within you – as does The Kingdom of Frog and the reason we all have been called to this place."

Suddenly, the crowd stopped their noise and a peace seemed to come over them. They felt a joy – his joy – and for first time some began to understand, even though they had been harsh to him.

But before they could say anything in response to a message they now could hear, Andy leapt from the cliff and jumped so far below that the crowd could no longer see him. He was gone.

Sophie gasped. She had no idea that Andy would EVER be gone or stop his wonderful teaching. "What would she do?" she cried inside.

All of a sudden she knew just what she must do. She would teach the message that she learned from Andy. She would help the other frogs overcome their fear and she would do all that she could do to help bring The Kingdom of Frog back together as one family, one tribe.

Howard sat on his perch above all of the activity below and smiled. He watched Sophie continue the work he had inspired Andy to do. Howard was very pleased and dreamed of what all of the future generations of frogs could become – and it was good.

Lightning Source UK Ltd.
Milton Keynes UK
UKHW051046110620
364721UK00003B/80

9 781489 728975